Hymns from the Heart

VERSES AND LYRICAL NOTES

ASHA IYER KUMAR

PARTRIDGE
A Penguin Random House Company

To order additional copies of this book, contact
Partridge India
000 800 10062 62
orders.india@partridgepublishing.com

www.partridgepublishing.com/india

To my master, my muse and my man

Contents

Foreword

In every publication there are certain contributors who become intrinsic to the style and image of the product. Their columns enhance the editorial content in tangible terms, and the publication and the writer grow in tandem.

Asha Iyer Kumar's weekly column is one such dimension to *Khaleej Times.* Not only is her style entertaining but also thought-provoking.

The arts and sciences have always been avenues where the milestones mark every interaction between the giver and the recipient. For writers like Asha, their words are their best bet for posterity. As a storyteller, life experiences are her grist and the combination of truth and imagination is where she delicately reflects the power and the glory of her pen. After an impressive debut with her novel, *Sandstorms, Summer Rains* in 2009 in which she painted word pictures of life, love and loss, she puts her creative elements into effective use again in her first book of verse, *Hymns from the Heart* that she compiled from her writings of just over a year.

Written as free verses, rhymes, quatrains and couplets, the book deals mainly with love and devotion, or shall we say, romance and spirituality, which in a sense are two sides of one ethereal emotion. To those who are romantically inclined, it will serve as love poems, and to those slightly exalted, it will appeal spiritually. There is a gentle thread of mysticism running through the work, and the wisdom of truth can be found in these profound and soulful verses of Asha's.

Read it at leisure. Read it one page at a time and let the beauty of her thoughts and words sink in you slowly.

Patrick Michael
Executive Editor
Khaleej Times

Introduction

I wrote my first poem when I was twelve and at that time I had no inkling that I would grow up to be a writer. Although poetry was my first love and I spent many years scribbling juvenile verses, I abandoned it for long, presuming that poetry primarily did not constitute a writer's life. I strayed as a writer for long, trying to find a grip here, a clasp there and a firm footing somewhere. In the midst of this meandering journey, somewhere I met and reunited with my old love again.

Ever since our reunion, I have been on a virtual cruise, suddenly finding seamless charm in all things bold and benign, dreaming during the day, waking in the night, spending hours in aimless reflection. This is what love and philosophy can do to you. It can make you a hopeless, silly sentimentalist. I am a little bit of both – a romantic and a philosopher, and this book of verses and lyrical notes is a manifestation of these wispy aspects.

The verses in this book essentially deal with matters of the heart and the soul. It sometimes becomes difficult to separate moments of love from that of spirituality, and the verses here will see an intermingling of these thoughts. I have divided them as 'free verse' signifying free stream of thought, 'rhymes' that symbolize the coming together of literary inspiration and expression, and 'quatrains' and 'couplets' that offer instant poetic gratification.

I present my "Hymns from the heart" for my readers to relish the simple flavours of poetry. May it grow on you like the effect of fine wine, leading you to that which makes you find love in all that you see, for boundless love alone can unify and sublimate the human race.

Verses

Poem of Love

Today, as I walked down the twilight trail
among the familiarity of seasonal bloom,
Skin swathed in the dimpled air of new rain,
The perspiring earth sedated, its rustic scent expended,
Somewhere among the common sights
I came upon Love, perchance,
Cloaked in pristine white,
Glistening in sundown charm,
Reflecting the elements in its misty eyes,
Humming to itself
a mystic tune of love that wet my cheeks,
wrapped me in its swirl;
Love that burst with sublime splendour,
Love that consumes the human spirit,
Beyond the flesh and its earthly demands,
Love perpetual, all pervading,
Unifying, inebriating, doused in mirth;
Today amidst the banal prose of life,
I met with a redeeming poem of Love.

From Where
My Words Emerge

From where do these words emerge?
Wherein lies the womb that begets these lines?
Is it from the bowels of my-self, the deep interiors?
Or from the vastness that lies outside?
Ah, folly, there are no two sides,
The expanse is one, only one,
Divided by a wall -
A wall of gooey flesh and inane senses,
A wall of concrete impudence,
A wall of many monikers,
Someday, the winds of wisdom
will knock it down,
And I will declare –
My words emerge not from here, not from there,
They arise from the wholeness of the sphere.

Tears and Rain

One, two, three,
And then in dozens they fell,
Soaking the face as I looked up the skies,
"Is this manna from heavens?"
Said my freckled cheeks,
"Sweet, unlike anything I have drunk,
If this be manna, drench me in it all life,
And spare me the brine of the skin and the eyes."

Out of Love

Yesterday,
As the inkpot tipped over a murky sun,
I fell out of love with you.
The dusk spread a smudge over
my scrambled thoughts about you,
The city lights torched my unsated love,
The deepening night charred my deserted eyes,
I wallowed in my secret abhorrence,
Drowning you, sip by sip in my drink,
And then, in a wild swill,
I declared you dead, as dead as a broken twig,
And so I went to bed.

As the day light broke,
You crept back into my head
and sank into the depths,
Breaking the walls of an obstinate spite.

I shall now wait for the night to fall
and bring a wick to reignite a smouldering despise
that dies and resurrects, ever again;
Alas! My days are dark without you,
And nights insufferable in your sullen presence.

An Ode to Pain

The sole way to live this pain
is to give it your name, my Beloved,
Snaking up cloyingly, to pervade my blood
and fog my veins,
Like the passions of a man drunk with besotted love.

The only way to bear this ache
is to fill it with your radiant hue, my Beloved,
Creeping up gingerly, to suffuse my days
and blind my view,
Like the rays of a dawn dunked in the new born sun.

The lone way to suffer this throb
is to play it as your lullaby, my Beloved,
Wafting up softly, to fill my sleepless nights
and drum up my breath,
Like the song of a nomad lost in the droning desert.

Yet,
Love me not so, haunt me not thus, my Beloved,
Smother me not with your nauseous closeness
that I should urge you to stay away,
Let there be distances in our love,
So that I savour the newer delights of my day.

To a Meteor

When did I implore that you stay with me?
I am no dunce to seize you from your fiery path
and strap you to my buttery body,
Nor seek a lifetime in your blinding presence,
Yet this much I implore –
Blaze into my space as you pass by,
And I shall arrest you in my eyes till eternity.

Tryst with My Love

Someday, perchance, if I meet you,
Will I know it's you, my Love?
Thrust into your anonymous presence
long I lived, unbeknown to your allure,
Ranting and chanting to your make-believe countenance,
Your existence a mere fallacy,
My love a deceit,
Our alliance a fabled lie,
Till I heard your mystic whispers
from the tiny crevices of my being,
Till you wrapped me in your gauzy drape;
Unrevealed, yet palpable -
Your presence resonates and your music rings
through the din of the day and calm of the night,
Someday, perchance, you materialize
in the winter white or the summer blaze,
In the autumn brown or the spring colour,
Will I know it's you, my Love?
If I know,
What in your blessed name will I do?

On the Beach

I love the spongy dampness
beneath my feet,
As I stroll with the sea breeze,
Picking up grains of sand on my wet paws,
Only to drop them a few strides yonder
and then pick new ones again,
They cling to me like fleeting moments
that wilt with my breath,
With me this instant, lost in the next,
Tiny specks of life move in step with me,
They fuse and fall like the folding wavelets,
Between the grains of sand that I gather
and the moments that wilt,
Is a journey that will last until the sun sets.

My Love for You

There is no flesh in my love for you,
No longing for the touch,
There is no desire for the limited pleasures
that stem from the skin,
Yet I long for you, my Beloved
I melt, I simmer, I vaporize,
I live in an undefined realm of passion
that asks nothing of you, except your constant presence,
Day after day I breathe your thoughts in,
Infuse them into my blood,
I gasp, I weep when you seem distant and hidden,
I wait for a sign, for a reassuring rustle,
And I drink my tears in joy
when you nudge me gently and say you are around,
In your love my life sustains
beyond my doubts and fears,
Let my contemplations on you be my prayers,
Let your thoughts about me be my blessings.

Romancing the Moon

Insane to fall in love with the mystic moon-
Perched in the firmament, light-years away;
Yet I confer with him as if he was only whisper distant,
Send him warm missives by soughing with the wind,
On lonely nights I sit by the lake,
Wait for him to appear in the placid waters,
And when he shimmies up to the surface like a sylvan spirit,
With trembling fingers I feel his rippled countenance;
Scorched by my warm, nimble fingers,
He melts and seeps into the thick folds of the night
and fills the crevices and corners of my being,
I whirl like a dervish, feeling his stirring presence
in slivers of the silver coated night;
When the mortal and the celestial merge into one,
The stars in the sky shower on earth,
Flowers in the forest watch in a trance, and
time freezes to witness a divine communion.

A Night with My Princess

O resplendent moon,
Let me take your place for a night
and watch my princess in her sleep,
Sneak into her chamber and be in mute company,
Give me a chance to wrap her in my silken shimmer
and spread my shade on her crimson cheeks,
When I wear your cloak and slip into her dreams,
Even the sentries of darkness would pretend to sleep,
If you think this body will give me away,
I will leave it at the doorstep and take my soul in,
I promise to leave before it is day break,
Let me take your place for a while,
Be her secret lover, and know the delight
that you indulge in so fearlessly night after night,
And when she awakes with the twittering dawn,
Will you tell her that it was the misty night
that left the dewy patch on her quivering lips?

Departure

When you arrive from the distant land,
You bring in a breeze with a scent that beguiles,
And sprinkle a hue that illumines,
I bloom in your presence, yield to your charm.

When you depart without a whisper
and vanish into an unknown space,
You leave me in a wheeze
as you steal my blush, my breath and my being.

Your absence only melts my heart,
But your departure chars my soul,
Why do you come if you have to leave?
Why do you bring in the whiff and fill me with it
If you have to wring my core out and deplete it?

Maiden in Waiting

The kohl in my eyes had dried up and caked
as I waited through the seasons,
And when I heard your footsteps on the threshold,
The rain clouds in my heart, waiting with me to pour,
Gushed down in a deluge,
Years of dark linings softened and smudged on my cheeks.

Now as I wait for you to waft down to me,
There is a tremor beneath my feet,
Why do these little moments feel so stretched?
Why is the distance from the door to my drape so long?
When you come, gently touch my kohl-stained face and say,
Did you weep for me, my dearest?
I will gaze into your eyes, and sigh -
This silver that tarnished with time,
Is waiting for you to shine it again.

Love's Grace

The expanse of love endears,
Its seamless frontiers beckon;
Alarming are its narrow constricts,
The limited confines and classifications;
The inhuman connotations and gimmicks,
The deformed versions where it festers as lust;
Stretched to its sublime limits,
Love is life's single purpose, its end,
and its quintessential grace.

Adieu

Come, let's walk down the dusky lane
before we bid the final adieu,
Let's stroll by the sea, and leave foot prints in its lap,
The tides will wipe them away, yet..
Let's watch the moon rise, and name the infant stars,
Day light will blot them out of sight, yet…
Let's sing a song, and leave our music in the air,
The blustering wind will sweep it away, yet..
Let's scribble our names on the city walls,
Coats of paint will cloak it over, yet…
Let's visit the antique store of our past,
We can't take them home to keep, yet..
Let's clasp the precious bits briefly to heart,
Time keepers will prise it from our hands, yet…
Let's walk down the dusty lanes once again,
Before the night swathes our old alleyways.

Absurd Love

Will I be chastised?
If I call out to the birds and the beasts,
To the stars and the seas,
To the blooms and the bees,
To the stone and the sand,
To every man that I meet,
To kin far and near,
To links feeble and fast,
Call out and let them know –
That I love them more than they would ever know.
World, will you be scandalized?
Will you stone me to death?
You will.
I don't blame you,
You haven't seen my Beloved,
My ecstasy is absurdity to you,
Someday you will know
when you catch His cherubic glimpse,
All I said was so utterly true.

Homecoming

After all my wanderings in the wilderness
I will return,
There is no place to go but your abode,
I am certain
to find you at the door waiting,
For this is my home, and you, my refuge.

Adultery

Is it adultery if I think about you, my Beloved,
When I am with my beau?
To love him, I must first drown myself in you,
Drink from your lips in my dreams,
It's from you that I learnt the songs of the soul,
It's in you that I heard the beat of my heart,
Without you, I would be a mere stump in his hands,
It's you that chiseled me into a sculpture with a breath
and a searing sigh to scorch his lips.

To a Creek

Who brought on
this surge of current in you, O creek,
These goose bumps on your skin –
It can't be the bristling winter wind,
That only chills and numbs the limbs,
It must be the silken caress of my Beloved
that makes you course so amorously,
It must be my Beloved's scorching kiss
that put a lilting tune on your luscious lips,
It must be his fervent embrace
that brought this blue glint to your eyes,
I watch with unconcealed envy
the fluid scratches he has left on you,
And beneath your coy surface
the love he has sown in you.

Many Moods of Love

Oh what a delight to behold
that each moment of my love
is so distinct from the other!
When the tumult of it has passed,
The calm reigns supreme,
After a tryst with the gross,
The subtle pervades the veins.

Lost at Sea

When I set out on a whim, mindlessly,
On a voyage into the open vistas of the sea,
Arms flailing with glee and hair lifting to the sky,
With no select course, no track to follow,
Little did I know, least the inkling
that a storm would blow and cast me away,
That wilful winds would lead me astray,
Far from the shore where my bulk lay in wait,
Now in the middle of nowhere as I lurch,
I shudder with fear at the chilling thought
that I might be lost forever if I persist,
Caught between the land that I love
and the expanse that lies ahead of me,
I bawl out in utter perplexity,
Will the skies open and speak to me,
Which way must I steer my stricken ship?

In Love with a Haze

"Are you in love with me?" asked the distant haze.
Deeply in love as any lover will be," said I.
"Insane you must be to love a nonentity,"
"Not so in my heart; in here you are a deity."

"Will you know me should I, disguised as man,
walk into your midst?"
"Promise that you will not, oh, promise me,
Not to profane my heart with your trickery,
Not to present to me what you are not,
For it's not a face, nor form that I love,
It's this haze that you are that I deeply adore.

On Separate Shores

Oh, what gross things divide us?
What crassness splits our single love?
Someday, I shall cross this physical sea
and fill myself with your infiniteness,
Till then, let us wait on our separate shores
with only our longing for company.

The Veil of 'I'

What eyes do I close to sleep?
What body do I lay to rest?
There is only a sense of a gauzy veil
that limply hangs on this notion of 'I',
The rest has succumbed to this lyrical silence
that you fill with your unseen presence,
There is nothing for the night to take from me
except this waste of a veil,
O night, take this, let this rag be your cloak,
While you cover your nakedness with it,
Let me rejoice,
For my soul is in the arms of my Beloved,
There, I melt like the full moon light
in the inviting arms of the sprawling dark,
With no eyes to put to sleep
and no body to lay to rest.

The Secret Lure

In the blue of the curling sea and of the sweeping sky,
There's a mystery that holds my eye,
Even the insight that all will die -
The clouds will dissipate and the waves sedate -
Fails to deter my probing of the wide,
There's a secret lure that the elements hide,
Is it your concealed countenance, O Love,
that makes me gaze at the vast faraway?

A Stranger in Town

Who are you,
They asked the stranger in town,
Flocking around,
Seized by his divine demeanour;
A mad nomad, said he,
Thirsty for the wine of love.
Bring me the drink, he cried,
Lest I die parched in my heart,
Beware, he said before they hurried,
If in a chalice I am served
I shall spurn it,
It's an ocean of love that I seek,
So that I may drown, not sip with my lips,
The townsfolk brought the ocean to him,
And together they drowned,
Descending into the immortal deep.

Staying Awake

Let me wallow in the dark,
I don't want to retreat into sleep
leaving my thoughts of you in night's sinister alleys,
For them to be waylaid by earth's evil vermin,
It's not in the viscous dreams,
But in my sound mindful state
that your face I want to find,
Though between this affirmed wakefulness
and the fluid realms of the unconscious,
What might be the distance, I fail to see.

I am..

I am no linguist with a surfeit of unspent words
that can split thought into a million shards,
Nor a scholar armed with serrated theories
that can mince the brain into a million chops,
I am no mystic with the aura of truant Gods
that can spin the body to a dervish dance,
Nor a poet stirring her heart's melting pot
that can froth over a thousand sensations,
I am a mere…I struggle to fathom -
Timbre in the air, quiver in the leaf,
Trickle in the heart, whirl in the brook,
A note in a refrain, a half touch of restrain
A wingless angel's whisper,
An unspoken love's embrace,
Or…. nothing at all, mere void
caught in a woman's flowing form.

Do You Remember?

Do you remember the day
when my words and your silence fell in love?
Look, they are still lost in deep embrace.
Do you remember the day
when your quietness responded to my inner voice?
I think it rained that day.
I can still catch the scent of the earth in my breath.

Starry-eyed

Last night I dreamed of a moving star and a meteor shower,
I caught them behind the drape of my eyes,
A gazing mirror said today,
"Oh, there's a new twinkle in your eyes. It's love, perchance."
I flashed an impish smile, winked and said,
"I am a maiden, starry eyed."

You and I

I am in love with your mind.
It's our shared thought that makes me believe -
There's no you, there's no me.

I am in love with your spirit.
It's our shared existence that makes me believe -
There's no God, there's no man.

Tale of the Gods

When man will creep out of his earthly lair
and elevate to heavenly heights,
His love will escape the grimy grounds,
From a worm to a butterfly he will change,
Then, I will scale the skies, ride the clouds,
Wear the cloak of the rainbow
and overflow with loveliness.
Looking down from above,
I will proclaim my love for you
through the lark's open song,
The rain will fall on your face,
Bringing my kiss to you;
The wind will sweep your breast,
Bringing my maiden embrace to you;
And the night air will wrap your feet,
Suggesting my intangible surrender unto you.
One day, man will know my love,
And know it as a tale of the Gods above.
Till then, I shall wait on these shores,
Scoring my quaint lyrical notes.

Mortal and Absolute Love

May it not that in mortal love,
Your passion weighs upon your beloved's heart,
Stifles the sighs of longing
and steals the magic of your union.

And in absolute love,
May it not that your passion
lies feeble upon your Beloved's bosom,
And failing to grow roots of promise,
shrivels and dies in His parched heart.

Drowned in the Sea

Let the space between us drown itself in love
and take us with it to the bottom of the sea,
Let the world believe we are split in death,
While we rejoice noiselessly,
Thousands of leagues under the rough, open sea.

You are That

You are that for which I have a hopeless yen,
Your name and form are incidental;
You are that which evokes infinite delights,
Your physical coordinates are peripheral;
You are that which invokes my sleeping muse,
Your manner and method are immaterial.

Nocturnal Song

"Nights are made for us,"
Chirruped a nocturnal creature,
For us to crack the secrets of the delinquent hours,
To unearth the allure of the mystic moments,
To caper in heady mirth alien to humans.
Nights are made for us,
Let's transcend sleep's monotony
and set out on a wayward journey
like drunken vagabonds on obscure plains,
Let's be distant partners in an unearthly banter
and lend our voices to night's silent cacophony,
For the nights are made for us.

A Flower's Love Notes

When you accost me, O black hued bee,
With your wicked buzz, under a Mayflower tree,
I shiver in bashful jitters, shimmy in seamless glee,
As you descend on me for a drinking spree,
I down my head, drown in an ashen sea,
With ruthless desire when you frolic on me,
In delirious love, I let my spirit free.

Drowning in Love

I am inundated
when I am in your presence,
My molten eyes run, profusely;
Oh, the sweetness of the stream
rinses my bosom,
And thence spring forth these mindless lines;
Tear me up with your fire, my Beloved,
Keep me awash in this burning ague,
Let me be doomed, drowned and dead
in this simmering pot of your glorious love.

Discourse

You are silent today,
Yet I hear your words –
In the rustle of silk against my skin,
In the patter of rain on my pane,
In the song of the sparrow on my sill,
In the puff of air in my breath.
When you are silent,
I hear your voice in all that speaks,
And when you speak,
All that speaks quiets down,
It's just you and me
and love's discourse between.

Song of a Vacant Reed

Where in this summer streak have you melded?
Where do I seek a trail of your passing?
In the hills and dales
or in the shimmer of the lakes,
In the wheeze of the wind,
In the gaze of the tulip
or the blaze of the forest fire,
Where in the lost citadel of love
has the glint of your eyes dimmed and died?
The song of my soul is bereft of words,
The faltering notes cry for reprieve,
I scour the void that transcends my skin,
Tapping my sagging soul, draining its sanguine stream,
Deranged and deserted,
I rip my stifled being into languid strands,
Looking for your trace
beneath the layers of a blinding night,
To find a sign
that to your presence will lead,
In the crevices of my cells,
In the heave of my chest,
In some sheathed chamber of my Self,
Aye, you exist,
Not in the openness of mountains and valleys
or in the folds of galloping gales
Or in the tranquil face of the lake,

But in my deepest ravines, in its secret caverns,
Yet the road to my instant core seems long winding,
And the stretch to your grace unending,
When did we beget such estrangement?
When did you shroud my heart with disdain?
Tear the curtain and come presently,
For in your absence, I am a vacant reed,
Depleted and devoid of song,
Come and fill me with soulful ditties,
And make me a crazed nightingale.

Love Notes

I don't seek the cheap thrills of words
in your pristine silences,
But let there be punctuations
that tell, there is life
in those deep, hushed valleys,
Where I wish to be a butterfly.

***

Can't our love be refreshed
with constant thought and memory?
Is love's steadfastness measured
only by the words we consciously utter?
Waiting for an answer
I stand by my heart's molten lake,
Watching it simmer, bubble by bubble.

***

If there was no honour to guard,
No bulk to preserve and life to save,
I would've been void,
I would've been love,
I would've been one with you.

***

Spring reigns eternally
over my land of love,
Where I meet my Beloved,
It drizzles all year long,
Look, my soul is scented
and my skin is soaked.

***

Unknown to yourself,
I steal you from your earthly dwelling
For my secret rendezvous,
Do you know
How often I meet you under the moonlit boughs?

***

A wafer thin breeze yesterday,
Crossed my path and faded away,
And I caught its passing scent.
The scent I caught yesterday,
Clings to my breath today,
Fearing it might be sighed away.

***

I am empty,
Yet I am filled with you,
Empty to my brim,
Yet filled to my core,

In my screeching absence
is your silent presence,
In you, just you, is life
and not a stir outside.

***

I stood alone in a crowd
till I saw you,
And in that moment, I melted
and became the teeming crowd.

***

I fear to profess my love for you;
I am a morning glory
waiting to wilt in the warmth of your arms,
You may take me to be a paper rose
to adorn your coat.

***

I loved for you many reasons –
the solitaires and sovereigns,
the dreams and desires granted,
It is passé.
Now my love is the reason, its own motive,
With nothing to seek, nothing to hold.

Passage of Time

I watch the passage of time -
In words scribbled on old scripts,
In portraits printed on faded sheets,
In the notes of a bygone lyrical piece,
In memories etched on a muddled mind.

I see the constancy of time
In the voices that have scratched,
In the passions that have waned,
In the creases beneath the eyes,
In breaths that have stalled.

As I gaze into the crystal ball of time,
Scrying all that Was, Is and Will be,
I think -
Does time fly on its wings?
Or does man sprint on his feet?
Between the mortal and the moment
Where lies the passing,
And where the truth of constancy?

A Broken Seashell

In a wooden jewel box
wrapped in silk
is a broken piece of seashell –
pale and rough-edged,
nursing its old wounds.

Somewhere on the sea bed,
Veiled by the waves
will be its counterpart -
iridescent and smoothened,
languishing in peace.

When did they break and part ways?
Why did I bring the fragment home?
Why do I save the severed relic in silk?
When will I throw the aching bit away?

A Walk in the Woods

Come, let's flee these scalding ramparts
of concrete summer and stifling surrounds,
Of teeming millions and sullied hearts;
Let's leave behind these affairs mundane,
This thrashing about in life's eddying strains,
Our lungs are weary from ceaseless gasps,
Come, let's take a walk down the trail
of yawning canopies and fresh foliage,
Draw in the scent of grass and greens,
Lose our hearts to the dew on the leaves,
Watch bees and butterflies gather honey,
Allow the breeze to caress our cheeks;
Let's waltz around like phantoms free,
Pause a while under sun dappled trees,
And from its perch when the nightingale sings,
Answer to it in like harmony;
Let's pick fragrant blooms along the way,
Chew at berries, both sour and sweet,
And when a thorn jabs at a heel
Swear at it and grimace like a child;
Let's scratch our names on the bark of a tree,
And wonder at nature's myriad mysteries,
When the rain cascades through the boughs,
Let's open our arms and embrace it,
And when the cosmos anoints us,
Merge for a while with the divine entity.

Rain and River Ditties

(1)

O seeds of monsoon,
As you pass over me enticingly,
I wish you will descend on me
and sow in me your sweet insanity,
You are the sea's suitor I reckon,
Yet won't you briefly flirt with me?

(2)

The rain brought down a million missives
from the steaming heart of the grey skies,
I drench in the unwritten words of bliss
and turn into a succulent poem of love.

(3)

What dampens the dame's restive eyes
and scathes her innards with sweltering sighs?
Is it the clouds pregnant with monsoon dreams
or the river sashaying with an earthly allure?
Is it the air soaked in mid noon's sultry streams
or her veins throbbing with love's essence pure?

(4)

The maverick rain and the mellow river
have wreaked havoc on a heart on fire,
What on this expanse has the vigour
to douse these leaping towers of flare?

(5)

All the heavens have descended in torrents,
And with them the deities,
Will the skies be bereft of divinity today
and the earth get beatified?

(6)

When a far away cloud
found repose in a river's heart,
The universe watched in stillness,
Then it poured,
And divinity opened her arms.

(7)

In the music of the monsoon,
Ring the many voices of rain –
The murmur of balmy drizzles,
The chatter of incessant showers,
The bellows of wild downpour;
When it falls it croons to me –

A story, a sermon or a symphony,
When it retreats it leaves behind –
A thought, a sentiment or a memory.

(8)

So brazen the love must be,
Of the rain man for the demure earth,
To maul her so ruthlessly
At the peak of the noon,
In the depth of the dark,
To mar her tranquility
with his passion's intensity.

So yielding the worship must be,
Of the earth for the maverick rain,
To allow him an unabashed run
on the swathes of her skin,
on the crevices of her being,
To revel in his wickedness,
And melt in his wild melody.

(9)

I hear the sweet song of the approaching rain,
I open my door to usher it in,
It drenches my doorstep and passes by;
Why didn't it cross the threshold
and shower on me for a wild rain dance?

(10)

The puddle in the path – reposeful and resting,
The stream on the sides – restless and running,
Between the two, where shall I choose to be,
A falling drop of rain should I ever be?

Word Games

I write neither for the present, nor posterity,
I scrawl to peel myself, constantly,
Someday I will arrive at my nucleus
and discover nothing,
Till then I will indulge
in these mind and word games,
It's the way I bide my time,
It's my secret route to the empty frontiers
of infinite freedom
and boundless bliss.

Lost, Found and Lost

Did it take so long for you to find me
or did you pretend I was lost?
When I was with you like day light,
You let me disappear into the wispy curls of dusk,
Now you return, seeking me,
As if the sun never set on us,
As if time had frozen
within the folds of life's tidal waves,
It was your folly then to let me go,
It will be a vice now to let you return,
Let us live on, on our separate shores
bearing the burden of our half love,
And watch the sun go down again.

When Spring Arrived

All year long I waited for the spring,
With verses to read and songs to sing,
With tales to tell and dreams to share,
All winter I chanted its name
lost in bated anticipation,
Alas! When it came draped in bloom,
Bewitched I stood - not a word, nor a whisper,
My songs, my stories, my verses, my dreams
quietly melded with its scented splendor.

Ache

The hope of your return
stretch these lingering moments to endless eons,
Someday I will freeze my love and crush my dreams,
I will shut the door and chide a raving heart,
Tell that you have found new pastures to stash your love,
My waiting will then bear no pain,
When the hope of your return will no longer remain,
Till then, let me wallow in this crushing ache
that keeps me alive day after day.

A Woman in Angst

Quiet! you mean, gurgling, mighty sea,
Stop laughing at me,
I haven't a stomach like you to swallow
the trash of life,
Have you ever been a woman?
A woman who is only a shot of vodka to a loveless man,
Only a rag doll to be torn asunder in repulsive lust,
A mannequin in his stable, a dancer serenading his
wobbling senses,
You are open to misuse, not me,
Stung by your saline aspect when he regurgitates you,
You roll down his feet,
Skirting and tickling,
You are shameless or lenient or coarse, or all,
You are made of a different element that accepts all,
I haven't the expanse to ingest the brine;
Yet I love, for the heart knows no restrain,
I love despite the pain and the disdain,
I will unload my woe from my heart in your lap,
Not my love for him, but his ugly name,
On your sands I will dig its grave,
Devour it and take it to your depths,
And let me live with the love, pure love,
With no wretched name to decor it.

Love's Tapestry

Should my hand break off yours,
Should my step fall behind yours,
Should voids and silences grow,
Should life become a bitter row,
Let's bend our routes,
Fork our ways,
Let's choose to say a happy adieu,
Meld into the world,
Disguise as aliens.
Let's drift light years apart,
Hide in the corners of the universe,
And then,
When the stars ordain,
Let's meet again
as strangers on a new shore,
and be lovers all over again.
Let's find virgin joys, pristine passions,
all unfound in an older sojourn,
Let's take newer oaths to be partners again,
till we fray in our hearts with the miles we tread
and our love falls apart from weariness,
And then,
Let's part and unite, part and unite,
Umpteen times, eternally,
For in our love's timeless tapestry,
Can the warp and the weft be left untied?

Rhymester

Someday,
The rhymester will drop her tools,
Her rhymes will fall silent,
The words from them will fall,
and float in the Ganges,
Like pilgrims' marigolds,
With only a cruising lamp
to lead the wanderer
to a land of still harmony,
Till then, let the lyrical streams run,
Washing up shores for miles unknown.

From You I learnt

You taught me to savour my moments
that, till then, I was devouring,
You taught me to linger in my moments
that, till then, I was hustling out,
You taught me to worship my moments,
that, till then, I was living out,
You taught me beauty,
You taught me peace,
You showed me a sound way to exist.

The Wax Ball and Fire

The wax ball implored the fire,
"Take me in your embrace and wrap me in your ague,
So that I may melt and be one with you."
The fire replied in its ocherous tone,
"I shall weave in your heart a wick, and touch its tip aflame,
It's for you to keep it aglow, and dissolve in my name."

Beauty and Love

The God of earth came to me and said, "Merge with me. I shall make you a gem and hide you in my bosom to be unearthed and adorned in a mighty crown."

The God of the skies said to me, "Meld with me. I shall make you a moon and pin to my bosom to be pined over and to embellish a poet's lyrical tone."

The God of the seas said to me, "Melt with me. I shall make you a wave and wear on my bosom to be surfed and caressed by the sunset's golden beam."

The God of the wind said to me, "Blend with me. I shall make you a fragrance and pat on my skin to be whiffed and caught by the blooming plots.

The God of the flame said to me, "Fuse with me. I shall make you a wick at the altar of the Lord, to be revered and kept aglow with the hymns."

None that they said I wanted to be, for in my unquiet heart rested a different dream.

The mighty crown will be vanquished, the poet's lyric lapse with time, the sunset's beam the night will consume, the blooming plots in winter will freeze and the hymns will fade with the holy sermon.

"Can I be peerless Beauty, which in the eyes shall forever remain?" I say.

"Nay, such Beauty in no firmament or earth have we lent to anything among our creations. Ask for else that we can bestow within the lines of human worth."

"Can I be seamless Love, which in the heart can forever stay?"

"Nay, such Love in no space between heaven and earth have we lent to anything humanly born."

Together in unison they intoned thus,

"To be Beauty and Love of proportions unlimited,

Raise and float above the meaner confines. Be our kin in our holy skin, and leave the coarse covering that in all things seek meaningless treat."

To which I say, "Make me a gem, make me a moon, make me a wave or make me a wick, make me any that will leaven me, for all I seek in this earthen stint is to be the silken soul of Love and Beauty."

"Ah, you seek Divinity, which in the garb of man or maid you shall not receive. Strive and rise, so you may someday, be the face of Love and Beauty, and ride on our wings to a never never land."

Thus saying, they drifted out, leaving a purple dawn on the fringes of my dream laden eyes.

Rhymes

What Are You, My Love?

At times you shine forth in my reality,
So real that I can see;
At times you flicker in my fantasy,
As gauzy as a reverie.

At times you pass by me,
So close that I catch a whiff;
At times you seem to be
perched atop a mighty cliff.

At times an object of my craze,
Tearing my soul apart;
At times a memory's bursting blaze,
Doused in my fluid heart.

What are you, my sweet Beloved -
A wispy thought, a vapour ring,
The sanguine hue in my blood
Or my heart's infinite suffering?

Home Everywhere

If home is where heart resides,
Where gentle love is sown,
Is there no abode besides
the ones I have grown?

I have left a bit of my heart
in places I have been,
Here a speck and there a part,
In vistas I have seen.

The lanes I have come so far
through the seamless wilderness,
Have slices of soul strewn afar,
Many speckled with tenderness.

I peer down the snaky road
that brought me well here,
And I see along the tracks I rode
a home for me everywhere.

If it's True

If it's true by you I'm loved,
Do me a favour, my Beloved,
You permeate my days
like sparklin' summer rays,
Now glide into my sleep
and descend in me so deep,
That I dream with your eyes
and breathe with your sighs,
One sleep between you and me,
and just one melting reverie.

Rainbow Man

You were traipsing across the sky,
When I caught you in my demure eye,
I held you in gaze for a fleeting moment,
And let you merge with the open firmament.

The brook on my way curbed her chuckle,
The trees suppressed a wayward giggle,
The lilting breeze stopped short of a tease,
I looked around, feeling ill at ease.

And when I stopped by a placid lake,
Tapped the snoozing waters awake,
I saw an iridescent hue leave my fingers,
And disperse green onto the water clingers.

Whence came the colours, I asked about,
It is not of my element, there is no doubt,
The blue in my eyes, the red on my cheeks,
The green I floated, the golden hair streaks.

Oh, I shrieked with sudden, bursting delight,
It's the rainbow man's amorous sight
that has swathed me thus in the vibgyor,
Like love's memory drawn from the yore.

Remembering a Love

I might have grown woods of love,
Yet in their midst thrives a grove
where the spring eternally thrives,
And the bloom of your love survives.

I might have found new lands to rest,
Yet among them is an old, woven nest
that roosts a past within its silken tufts,
Holding me above life's deepest troughs.

I might have soaked in myriad passions,
Yet amidst them linger faint impressions
of glances coy and love's touch searing,
And the brimless pools of eyes tearing.

I might have walked a world's expanse,
Yet on your earth is the stamp of a stance,
Bearing witness to a hesitant liaison
that began and ended for no good reason.

The Tree and the Shade

I stand wavering, undecided, to choose
between the tree and its murky shade,
Hard pressed to work out an amicable truce
in the heart and mind's constant crusade.

Shadows that proffer shelter in the light,
Vanish as the day beats a dusky retreat,
Tree with its wealthy spread and height,
Stands to support on its firm sturdy feet.

Yet the trustless black silhouette I embrace,
Heedless to the birds that come to nest,
In the ephemeral comfort I find my space,
And discount the tree, my final place of rest.

Seeking Grace

Round and round in circles,
My tainted self wanders,
Looking for earthly miracles,
A breathing stump meanders.

Breeze that passes, like a sieve
through my heart, to gently sift,
With each wheeze that I heave,
My sullied brook and take the silt.

The raking wind is a redeemer,
Whom I accost with open arms,
Like an unfettered streamer,
Yielding to its gusty charms.

Will someone please tell me
the name of the sacred place,
Where the river meets the sea,
And obtains the divine grace?

Differences

Smile wears many a heady hue,
Laves faces with sweet fondue,
Why do rolling tears have but one
colour and shape that spare none?

Thoughts that occur in one and all
have no breaking language wall,
Why then do men have dialects,
And countless names as sects?

Love that inspires every heart
has no border to tell apart,
Why then does hate echo sound
that leaves sweet sanity unwound?

Half Open Heart

Let the window of your heart stay half closed,
Let the charms that you hold lay half disclosed,
For love to peek and sigh in thought
and to covet that which is unsought.

Unguarded if you let passion sweep in,
Weariness will thrive, the lure wear thin,
Let there be a guaze between your closeness,
And intrigues galore to fuel your lovingness.

The Source of Joy

Is it the black of the cloud that I love
or the gleaming gray of the rainfall?

Is it the dark of the dusk that I love
or the tender tint of the nightfall?

Is it the brown of the earth that I love
or the sundry shades of leaves in fall?

Is it the sprint of the river that I love
or the deafening descent of the waterfall?

Is it the stretch of the lips that I love
or the tumultuous tears of mirth that fall?

Is it the kiss of my beloved that I love
or his grasping gaze that makes my eyelids fall?

Is it the sacred hymn that I love
or the mystical master who checks my fall?

Where lies my heart? Whence comes the love?
What presents me with this joy's windfall?

Sacred Hymn

Between the velvety dark
sequined with starry delight,
And an air of silence stark,
What shall I choose tonight?

The shroud of black frightens
with sinister secrets stuffed,
The calm of silence enlightens
a heart with passion puffed.

In the stillness that pervades
behind ceaseless insect sounds,
There's tranquility where fades
a mind that anguish hounds.

I filter the drone of pests,
Wade across the lurking dark,
To where obscure quietness rests
and spot a glowworm's spark.

In a noiseless realm I merge,
In a fathomless ocean I swim,
Ah, my soul stands on verge
of singing love's sacred hymn.

Driftwood and Flotsam

Said the driftwood to the flotsam,
"Whence do you come here?"
"Fleeing from a sinking ship
I lost and found my way here."

"Blessed are you to break away
from the steely bulk and crew,
You now float unrestrained
in the vastness of the blue."

"Of which land are you a native?
Is this your place of stay?
Are you a chip of a wasted tree
or a guileless chunk of clay?"

"Of where I had my origin,
There is no memory left,
From times I can imagine,
This salt is where I rest."

"What stories do you bring
from places you have been?
Have you glided down a spring
and seasons have you seen?"

"Ballads to share I have many,
But swear upon me a thing,
Tedium should you find any,
Hint and I'll no more sing."

"Undeterred, may you chant,
With all my heart I'll listen,
Sickened by the worldly rant,
I seek to escape the prison."

"You echo my inmost thought
and unveil my shrouded side,
As if you have secretly caught
the lunacy that lurks inside."

"Is it chance that brought us here
to meet upon these waves?
Let's cruise to the sublime sphere,
It's all my heart now craves."

"Be my mate in this expanse,
To nameless havens we'll float,
Like drifters waylaid by a trance
to explore reaches remote."

Thus bobbing in supreme glee,
A flotsam and a driftwood piece,
Scripted on the folds of the sea,
A quaint tale of love and peace.

Should You Leave, My Friend

Should you ever choose to separate at your wanton will
from the wholesome picture of our hearts' goodwill,
Know this, that despite our affinity's immature death,
My soul in its vacant place will bring no new breath.

For on the canvas with hues that I had merrily filled,
The space I've bestowed you is not mean or frilled,
Not a mere streak of paint that follows an errant path,
Nor a fleeting contour of layman's passion or wrath.

Should you ever choose to leave these fragrant lanes,
Know this, that I shall find you in my memories' plains
And in the lush meadows of my frequent, lyrical strains,
For in your company, I sought no coarse carnal gains.

In the vastness of the sky, in the dreamlessness of sleep,
In the shallow spaces of the mind and its hidden deep,
In all that flashes and fades in the simmering day light,
In the crevices of a speechless, pensive night.

Should you ever choose to depart my colourful image,
Know this, I placed less merit on the curve of your visage,
Nowhere will you remain concealed from my inner eye,
For objects sublime like you are not lost, nor do they die.

In the painting of life, a long way down in the ripe years,
If not as vivid strokes of colour your presence appears,
I shall grieve not, for man and muse are wholly disparate,
The former has demise, the other lives to a timeless date.

Should you ever choose to split and find your cosmic way,
Know this, I shall not, by plead or force, make you stay,
And if, in the madness of our palling forever you will
remain,
Know this, it will be an endeavour for our hearts'
mutual gain.

Love in the Wilderness

I want to grace the deep shadows of the hills,
And gather in my skirt the hue of the meadows,
Listen to the tales your silent lips will tell
From behind the whispering towers of the pines.

I want to wander in the openness of the skies,
And scatter my desires in the lap of the plains,
Sing to the slumbering quietness of the nights,
In a voice echoed by the sweet nightingales.

I want to catch your scent in the wan twilight,
And dunk my drunken spirit in your quivering quiet,
Sow seeds of passion that in earth's womb will lay,
And sprout a wood of love that forever will stay.

I want to merge with the space that you pervade,
And be a misty dame in your feverish embrace,
Conquering the dubious fence that sets us apart,
Nestle in our love, and fade with the morning star.

I want to break the fear that rims my crazed heart,
Raze the walls of conceit, these limited confines,
And be that, that with its thousand hidden fins,
Wades in the ocean of peerless love that you are.

Summer and the Desert Lass

He crept in with his feetless clandestine steps,
Phantom like, with fire in his cavernous throat
That with each exhale singed her supple skin,
And gave the smoulder in her heart a new flame.

Oh, in what numerous manners does he torment
this desert lass, with his hushed malevolence,
Stirring and churning her blood that escapes
the skin, leaving behind their sanguine tint.

Is it with dread or obscured love, I cannot say
that she watched him swamp her guarded terrain,
Like armies advancing into the enemy's domain,
Leaving her long held defenses in utter disarray.

To his glowing grip in the day, and sultry charm
in the night, the desert lass falls hapless prey,
Soughing through the afflictions of her obsession
for the intruder who thawed her heart's lingering chill.

She fills her sandy dunes with her cryptic love songs
that the summer man croons as he scorches her core,
Sniffling now, smiling now, behind her demure veil,
Lost in the pain and pleasure of her cloying new love.

Days of torrid ardour will soon expend, she reckons,
The crimson blush on her cheeks will in no time fade,
For the summer man is a nomad with blasé sentiments,
Pandering passions at will and slinking away.

Yet, she delights in his transient presence, simmers,
Harvests moments of ecstasy and tucks in her heart,
To warm her winter shivers and doleful days,
And to douse the suffering of his going away.

An Ode to Silence

At times, I stand in thrall of thy covert charm,
At other, I cower in the shadows of my alarm;
What deep intrigues thou hold within thee,
That at once beguiles and frightens me?

Amidst the din and deranged cacophony,
How do thou keep such collected harmony?
The more I attempt to fathom thee,
The more thou seem a bottomless sea.

My love for thee is an inscrutable irony,
In thee I hear the strains of a symphony,
In thee the noiseless stabs of apathy,
And in thee I find my voice's empathy.

Resurrection

When the searing winds of love sweep across,
Wedging the drossy mass and elements gross,
The wick of sedate breath that flickers within,
Drops its demeanour, rages and razes the skin.

Cremated by your celestial love, this heap of ash
revives like phoenix, rekindled by a lighting flash,
To be fanned ablaze by your arduous swirls,
Burnt and restored, ever again in passion's whirls.

Quatrains

When I reflect on love
No face shows in my eyes,
But deep in my heart I know,
That facelessness is you.

***

Despite its searing flame,
I adore the ominous fire,
It's a love that spans
a non-physical plain.

***

The biggest fear men bear in life
Is losing those they greatly love,
Yet this lonesome sorrow is rife
With no dread to straddle above.

***

The sweat of summer wraps my skin,
Reminds me of soaking in a deluge akin,
One from a restless melting within,
Other that rinsed a passion therein.

***

The dreams are so real,
And the days so surreal,
I wonder where shines the light,
And where the shade of night.

***

At times I feel so fluid
that I fear I might flow away,
At other I feel so hinged
that I fear I may grow root in clay.

***

When the song of the swan
serenades the silence of the lake,
Stars from the skies come down
in the guise of gleaming snowflakes.

***

I loathe the wanton words that steal
my mystery from the heart, and reveal,
Someday with stolid silence I shall seal
the voice of my mind's unceasing spiel.

***

Watching a relationship grow
is like taking a walk in the woods,
Watching it moulder to dust
is like being on a sinking ship.

***

If the muse that inspires,
In flesh someday transpires,
What poem shall I write,
Dazed by its blinding light?

***

Even after I rose to the clouds' height,
The skies seemed so distant to my sight,
At what heavenly altitude should I glide
to catch a glimpse of the faraway guide?

***

It is my love's greatest discovery -
From the way you dwell in my mind,
That you may be more obsessed of me,
Than my heart, of you, might ever be.

***

There is a lingering reality
between me and my-self,
With what eye do I perceive,
That which fills this vicinity?

***

Those magical moments,
When in sagging weariness,
I lean on the grand emptiness,
And it holds me up like a wall.

***

When the faults in my strokes begin to rile,
I spread the canvas beyond the skies,
In the vastness that I see in my eyes,
The asymmetry pales into inconsequence.

***

My love for the glowworm's glimmer
rests above the full moon's shimmer,
Oh, the sparks of fleeting life endear
than the chalky night's constant smear.

***

From nothing it came,
Into nothing it will fade,
Yet this vain, flimsy moment,
Swaggers like it is eternity.

***

The fragrance I caught of
you from miles away,
Brought memories of another nameless love,
And in the name of that unearthly faith,
I lost my earthly heart unto you.

***

Love will seek reason
When the madness in it dies,
And for the madness to die,
Love must first die.

***

I am the pilgrim,
I am the journey.
You are the deity,
You are the destination.

***

Every time the pestilence of life kills,
My soul travels to that secret abode,
Where in the presence of our bodiless love,
I am revived to be embodied again.

***

There is no fear in my love for you,
For in it, I seek to rise and not fall in grace,
Yet there is fear in my love for you,
For in it, I seek to win and not lose my face.

***

What ballad do I sing of my celestial love?
Shed your mortal cloak, and wear your wings,
To meet me in the aerial sphere, beyond boundaries,
There, in my unbodied embrace, know my celestial love.

***

The stars are the secret desires I whispered in the twilight's ear,
The rains are the tears I shed on the cloud's spongy shoulder,
The winds are the breath I sighed into its sprawling lap,
The spring blossoms are the ballads I sang into the winter air.

***

The summer that scalds the air outside,
Seeps in to singe the room inside,
Oh, what breach in the bulk that separates the two spaces,
Allows the fire to invade the inner reaches?

***

When God's silence gets too loud,
The raving man quiets down,
And then takes place a discourse –
Unspoken, unbroken and unheard.

***

These undulating waves of contemplation,
That as lines of verse washed ashore,
Made an oyster rise from the deep,
And befriend a beached sea urchin.

***

Every emerging thought of you
Becomes a floating verse,
I find you in my pool of thoughts,
And lose myself in the sea of rhymes.

***

The wings of waiting are weary today,
Let them descend into sleep slumber;
The dawn will see them soar again,
Till they break and plunge in pain.

***

Is my love a return on your giving?
Or is your giving a reward for my love?
Who is the giver? Who is the taker?
Between us, can we not just love?

***

I walked the street
as the sun went down,
Looking for the alchemist
who brought the gold to town.

***

In poetry is my heart's speech,
In prayer is my soul's search,
Between the two are pristine silences
that I blot with mundane utterances.

***

In your absence,
I am lost in a jungle of strife,
Without you,
It is not even a lie, leave alone a life.

***

Before I met you,
I acted, sang and danced;
Now that I have you,
I play a symphony.

***

The slighter the view, the greater the insight,
Sometimes I wish I were blind,
So that I could gaze behind the eye,
And discover the unseen vistas of life.

***

Find me a place to dump this crazed heart,
These ramblings upon a storm lashed shore,
Will you offer me a resting spot
to bury my chest and its wild cravings?

***

The thoughts I float through my words
are only whiffs of a deeper scent,
The rose that stores the fragrance
lies wrapped in an inner silence.

***

You resided in the words that I scrawled,
Now you dwell in the gaps in between;
I conversed with you with gilded sounds,
Now I contemplate on you
with silence pristine.

***

On nights of bleak, new moon,
I seek out a ray of silver light,
On nights when the orb is bright,
I stay indoors and moan.

***

Perched on the tallest branch,
The falcon is raring to go,
But its feet are ensnared
in the boughs and berries below.

***

Couplets

My love for you has disintegrated,
I now find it scattered everywhere.

***

Whether in spate or sedate,
An undertow keeps a river in state.

***

If silence breathes its last,
How will I ever know?

***

I can't lug home all that I love,
Knowing this, unrestrained, I love.

***

The heart of love, I haven't seen,
Beholding its feet, I yielded therein.

***

When silence opens its mouth to speak,
Each word that spills becomes an epic.

***

To whom silence is an ensemble,
What ornament can words resemble?

***

The desert dame dances in an oasis patch of
time,
Like a dervish she swirls to her Beloved's
silent rhyme.

***

In this love that kills me,
I seek my way to eternity.

***

Lovers and lunatics – just let them be,
Their true ecstasy, can the world ever see?

***

Someday, when I meet myself,
I shall know my true story.

***

For a driftwood in constant transit,
What sense do 'here' and 'there' consist?

***

From one end, everything matters,
From the other, nothing.

***

Let the pristine truth remain,
Don't utter it and render it vain.

***

Why does my tenuous fear of you
usurp my intense fervour for you?

***

Can the caterpillar know the nectar's sweetness
if it doesn't escape the cocoon's closedness?

***

Did time seize my love and lock it in this moment
or did my love embrace time and attain eternity?

***

Someday,
When the fire in my heart razes me down,
Will you blow a breath to revive me again?

***

If all that's smothered in the chest, be carried to the
earth,
Will the dirt bear the saddle, of our woes that began at
birth?

***

For unspoken dialogue to happen between two distant
shores,
There must be an unfathomable ocean of love betwixt
the two.

***

If your missive of silence is replied with my verse of quiet,
Will you read it in the calm of your heart?

**

What love cannot, can life ever be?
What the master cannot, can man ever be?

**

Teach me to shun this temporal love that ends,
And fill me with one that to infinity extends.

**

Won't you accept me and embellish your heart, my Beloved?
Even the cactus adorns the living rooms of many a rich
man's house.

**

Will the moon that glows on the largesse of the sun,
Ever have a rendezvous with her towering patron?

***

I am just a madman's song,
A stream that springs from somewhere unknown.

***

Are you an apparition or an actuality?
Is my cryptic love for you a frivolity?

***

Everything that my eyeballs can see
Is a metaphor to an unseen reality.